Peggy Louise Parrish
Parma. Idaho
Cover pictures and interior artwork were
created by Peggy Louise Parrish

ISBN-13: 978-542924672
ISBN-10: 1542924677

Printed in The United States of America

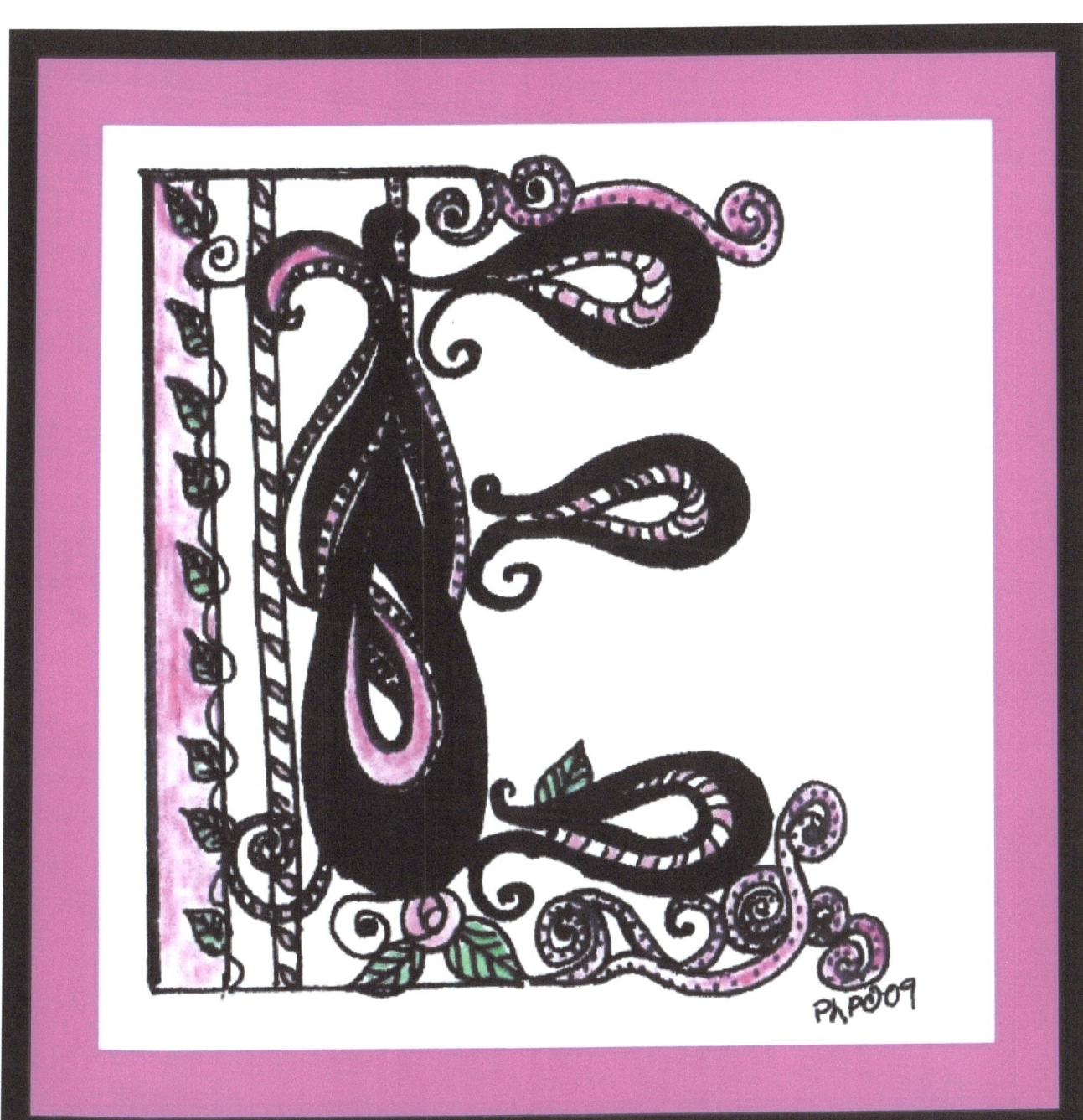

The Elegant Letter E

Coloring Book

By Peggy Louise Parrish

C, 2017

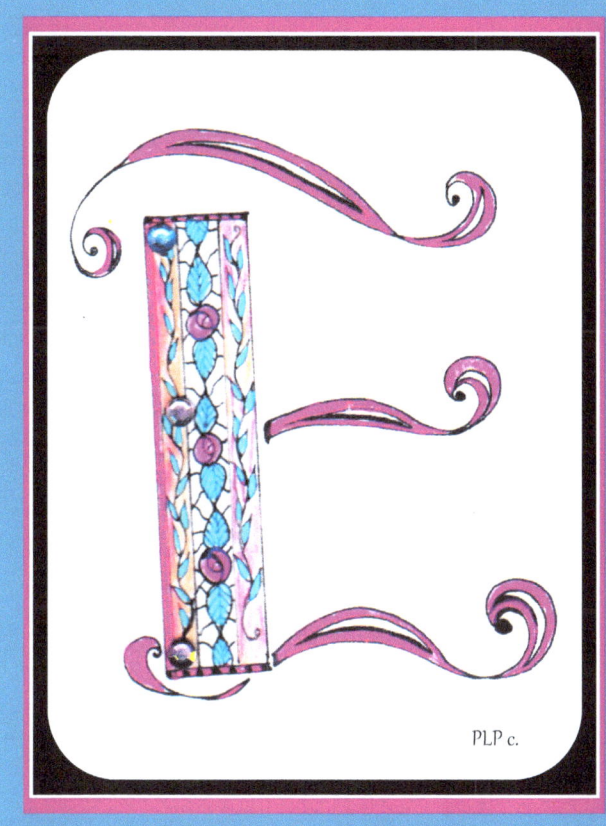

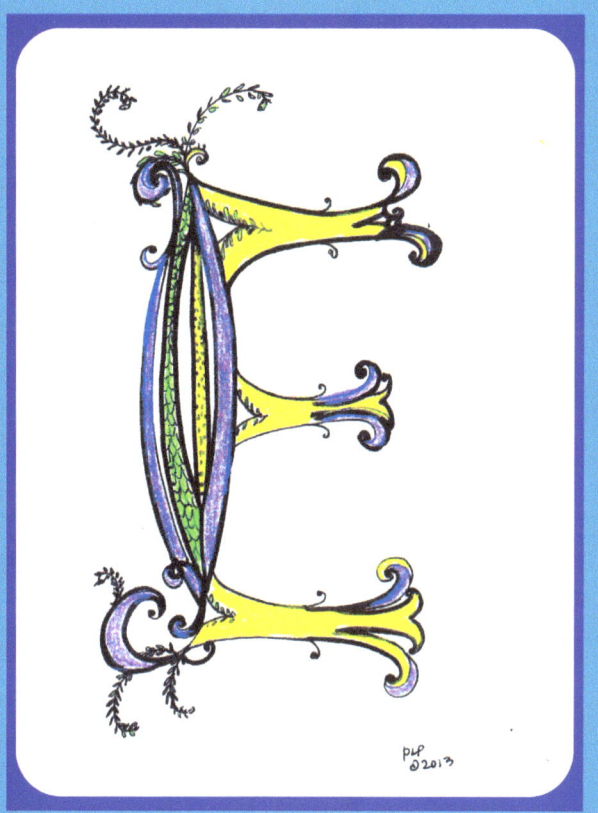

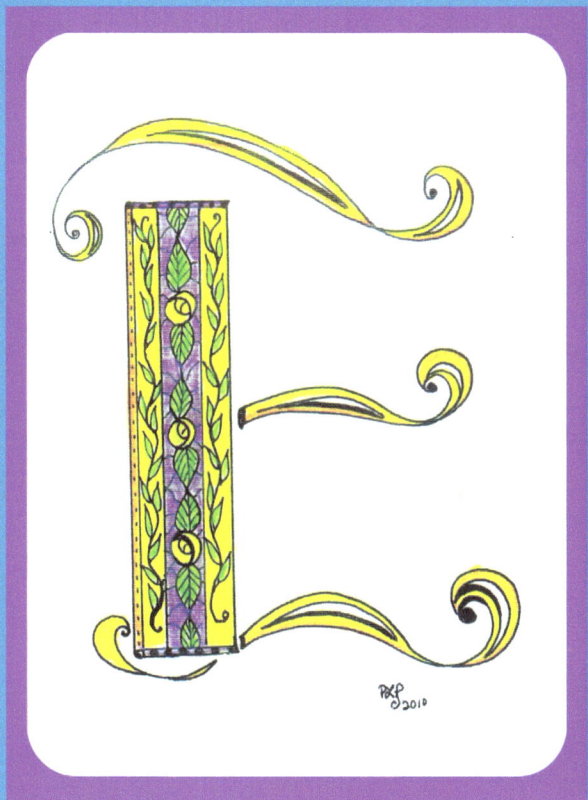

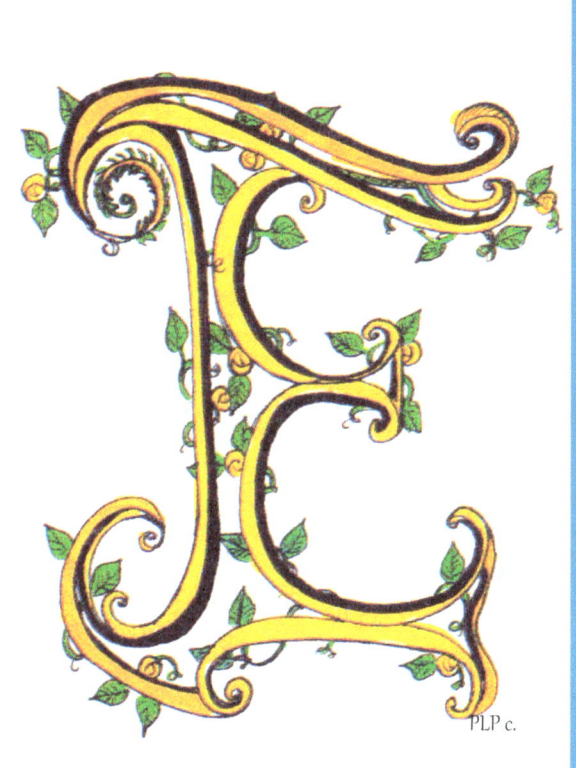

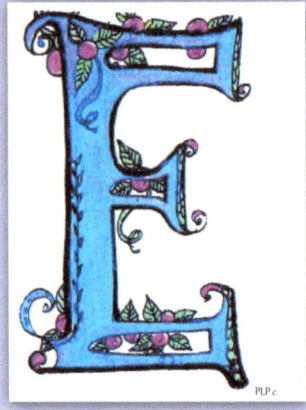

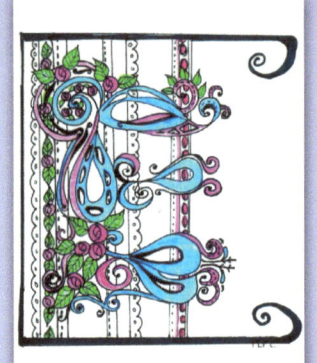

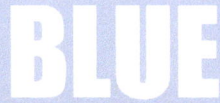 BLUE

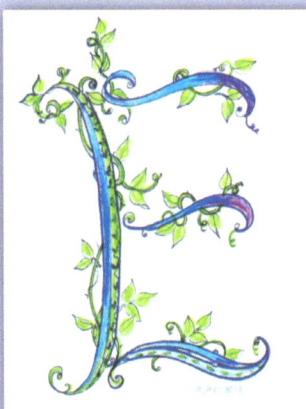

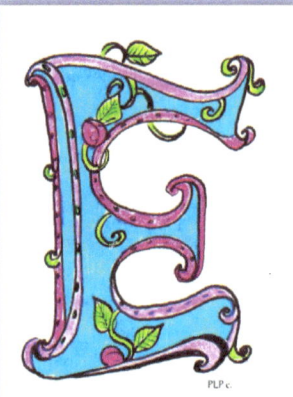

Can Be

So

ELEGANT

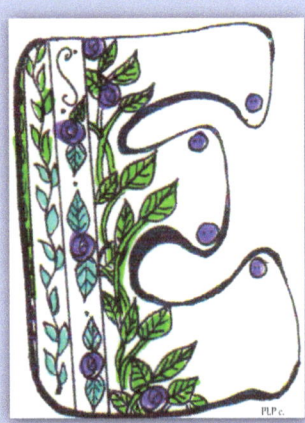

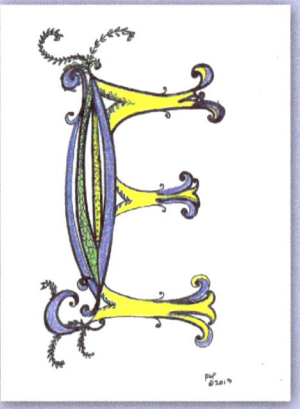

Dear Coloring Artist.

I had great fun designing these E letters. I hope you will have a great time choosing the colors you think they should be. There are a few pages of some of the ways I chose to color some of them. Quality colored pencils work really well . If you do choose to use watercolor pencils, markers or paint of any kind please remember to place a scrap paper behind the page you are on.

Perhaps your first or last name begins with the wonderful letter E. Or maybe a friend of yours has an E name. You may make a few "in house' copies of any page that you want to try in different colors. I only ask that my initials are left(PLP) and that you do not sell anything with the letters. Surely giving one as a gift would be a great blessing. You may want to use glitter or add in or around the letters with something you think up.

Letter Coloring Therapy might be so enjoyable that you want to try some of my other letter Books. Have fun!

Art creator, Peggy Louise Parrish

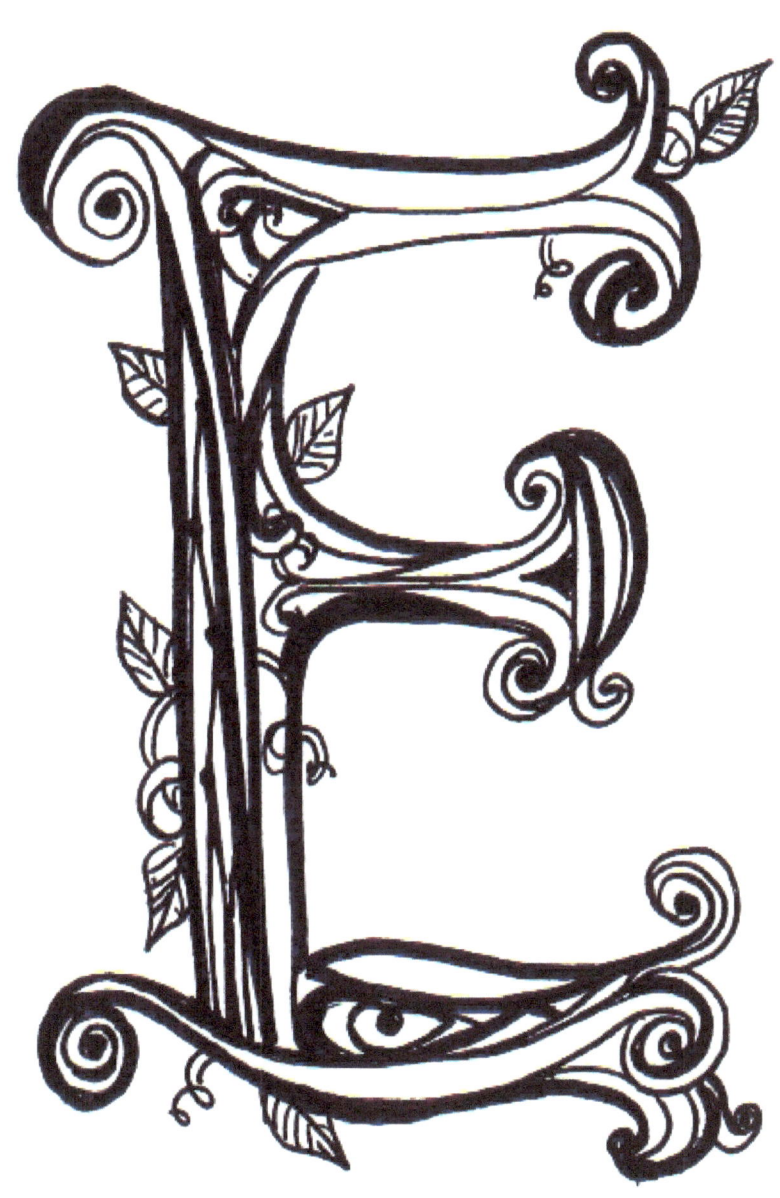

PLP c.

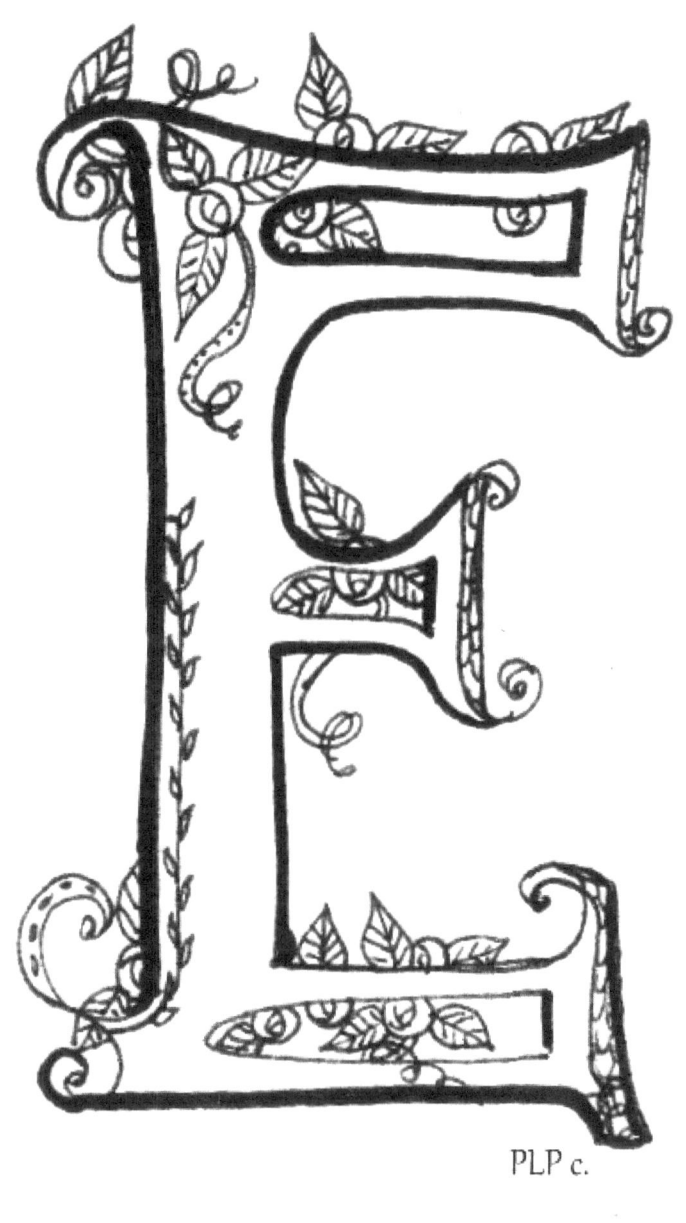

PLP c.

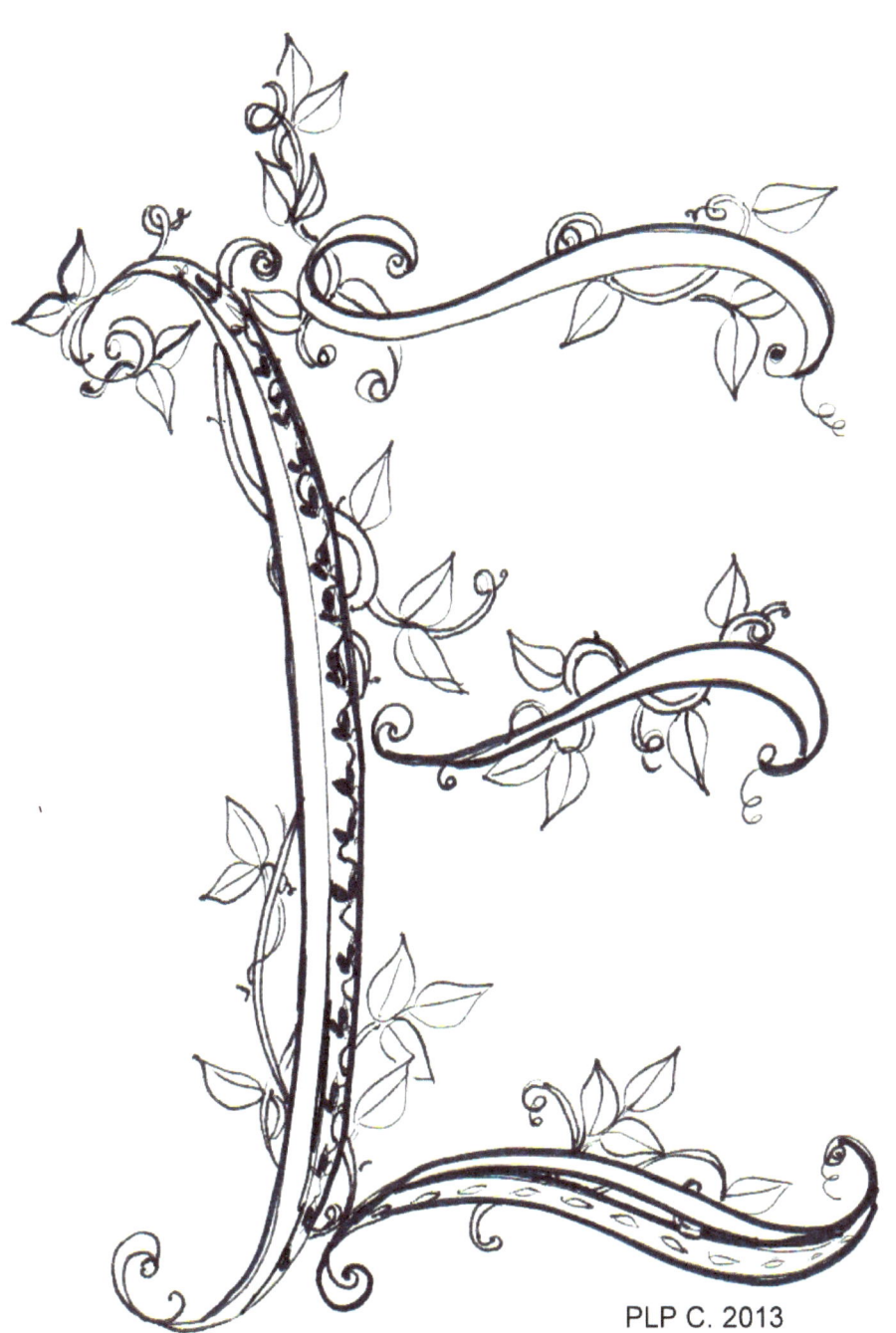

PLP C. 2013

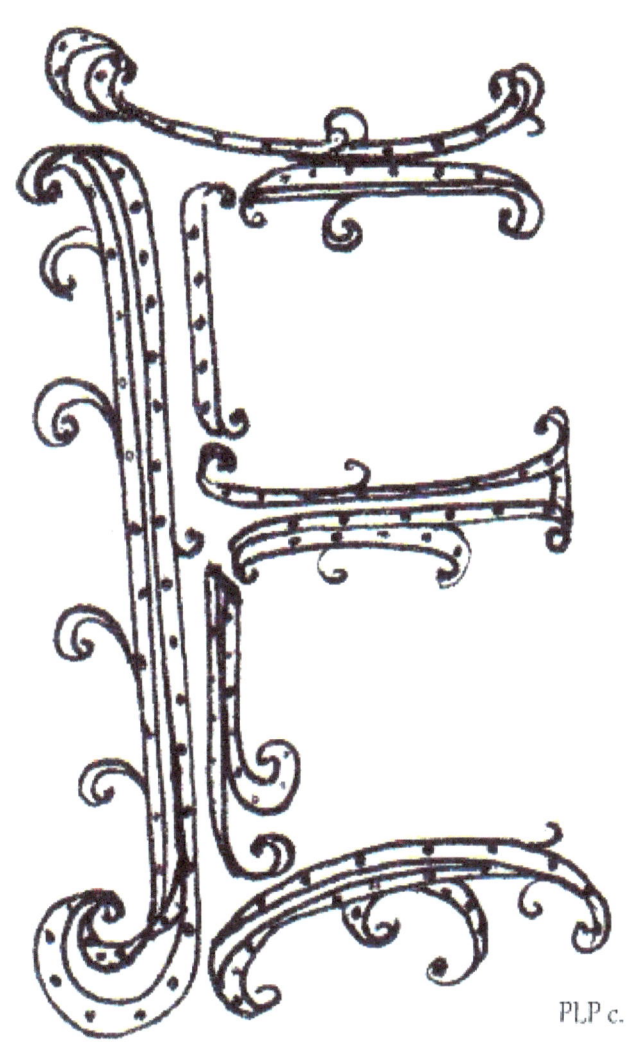

PLP c.

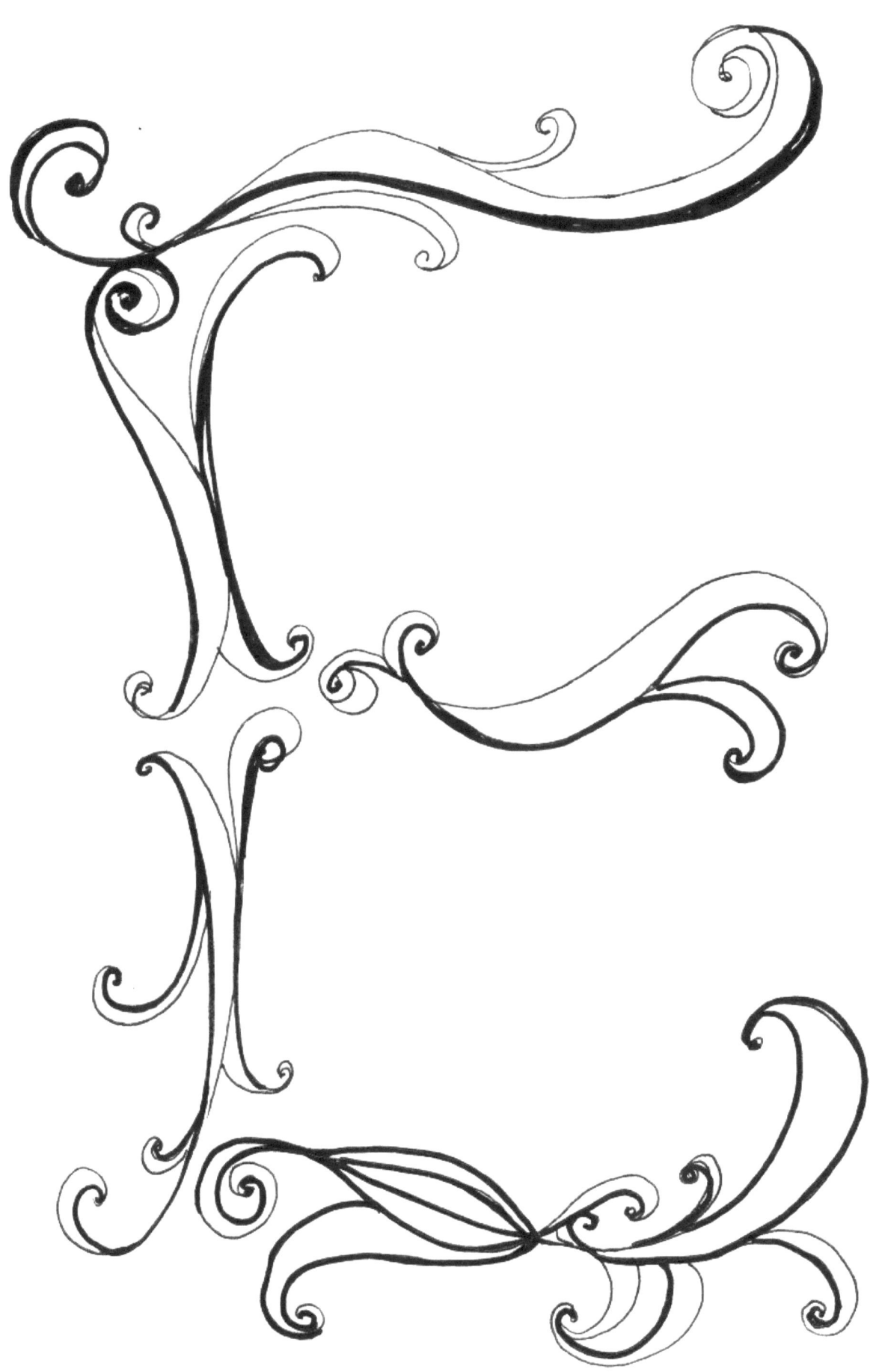

PLP c.

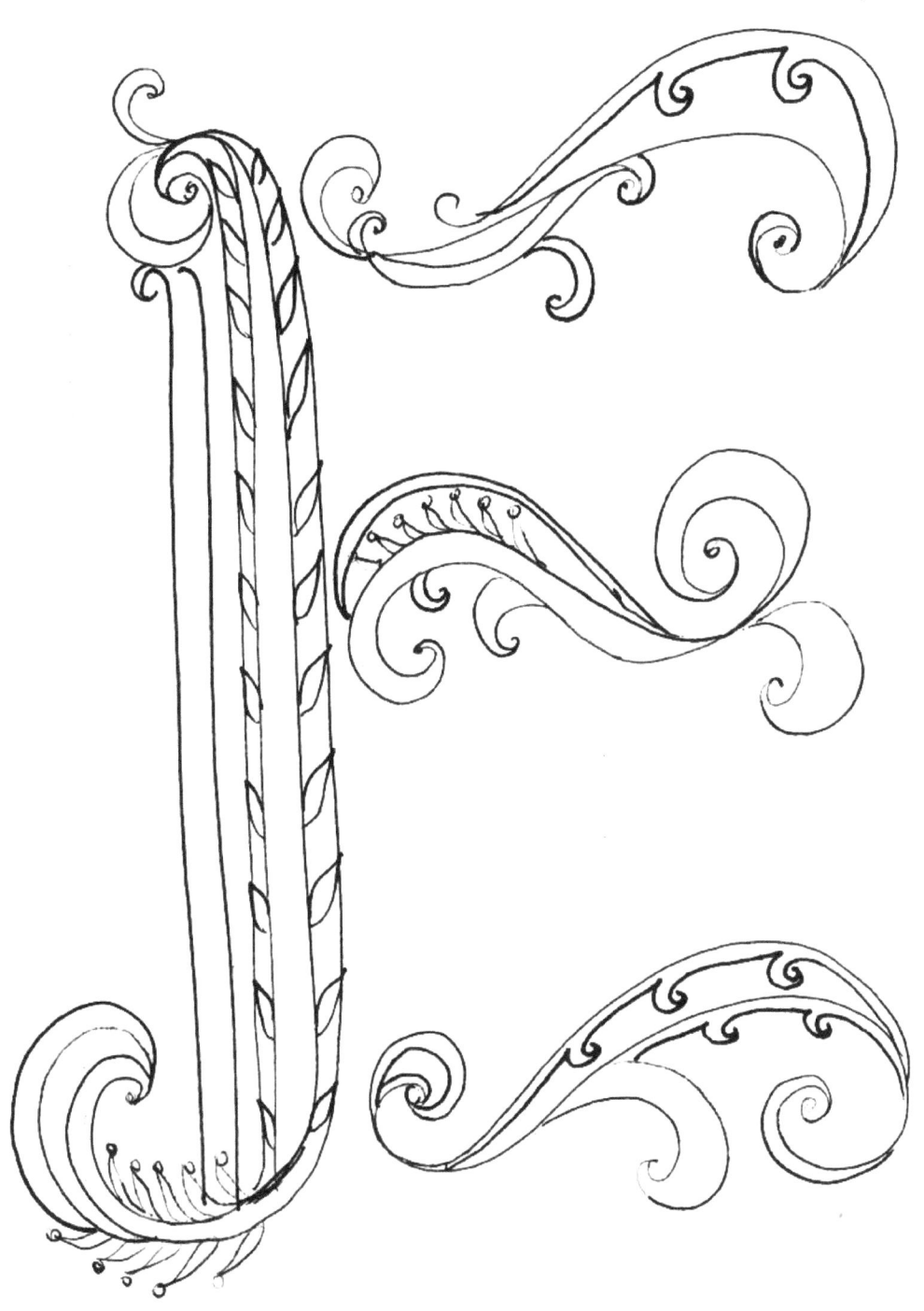

PLP c.

PLP c.

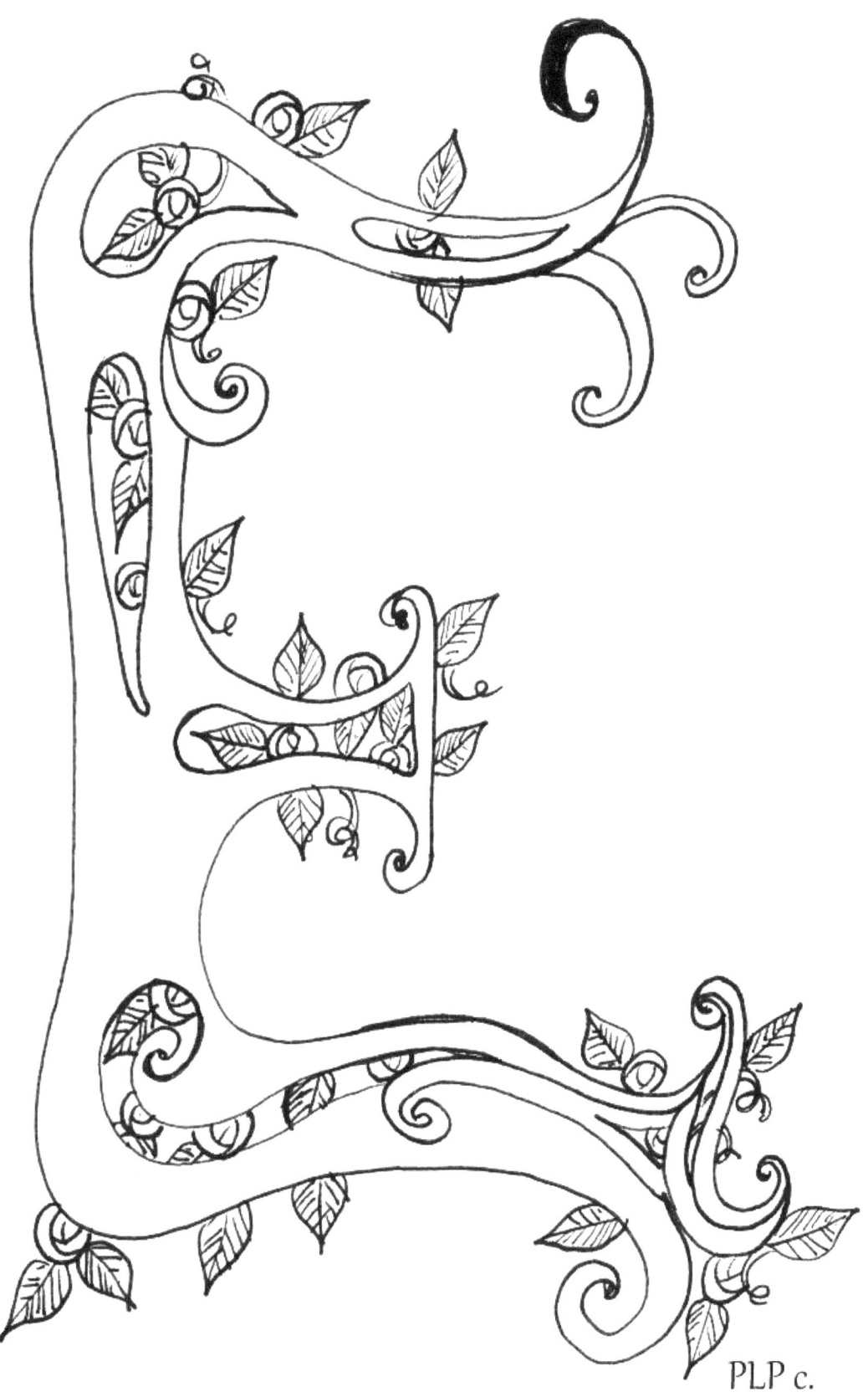

PLP c.

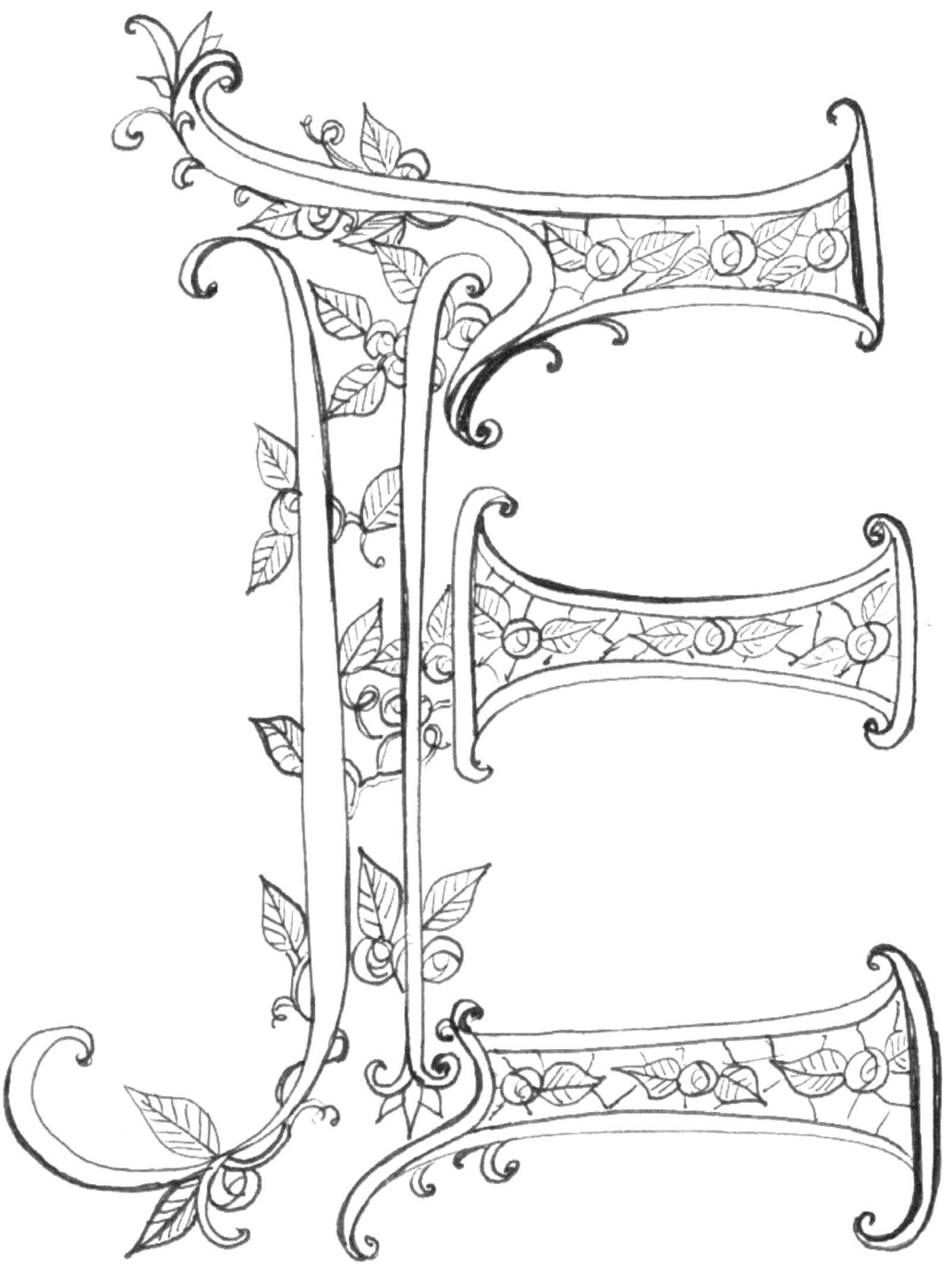

PLP c.

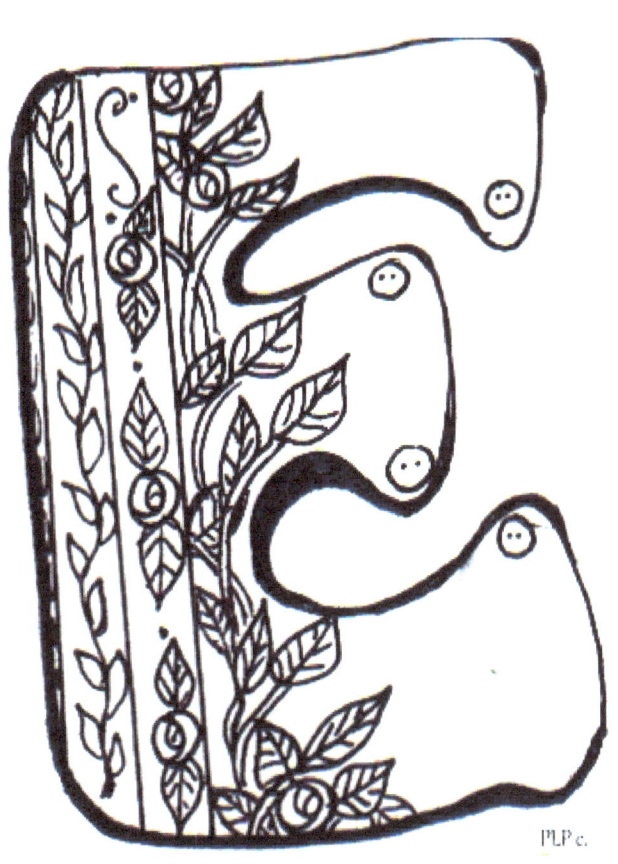

PLP c.

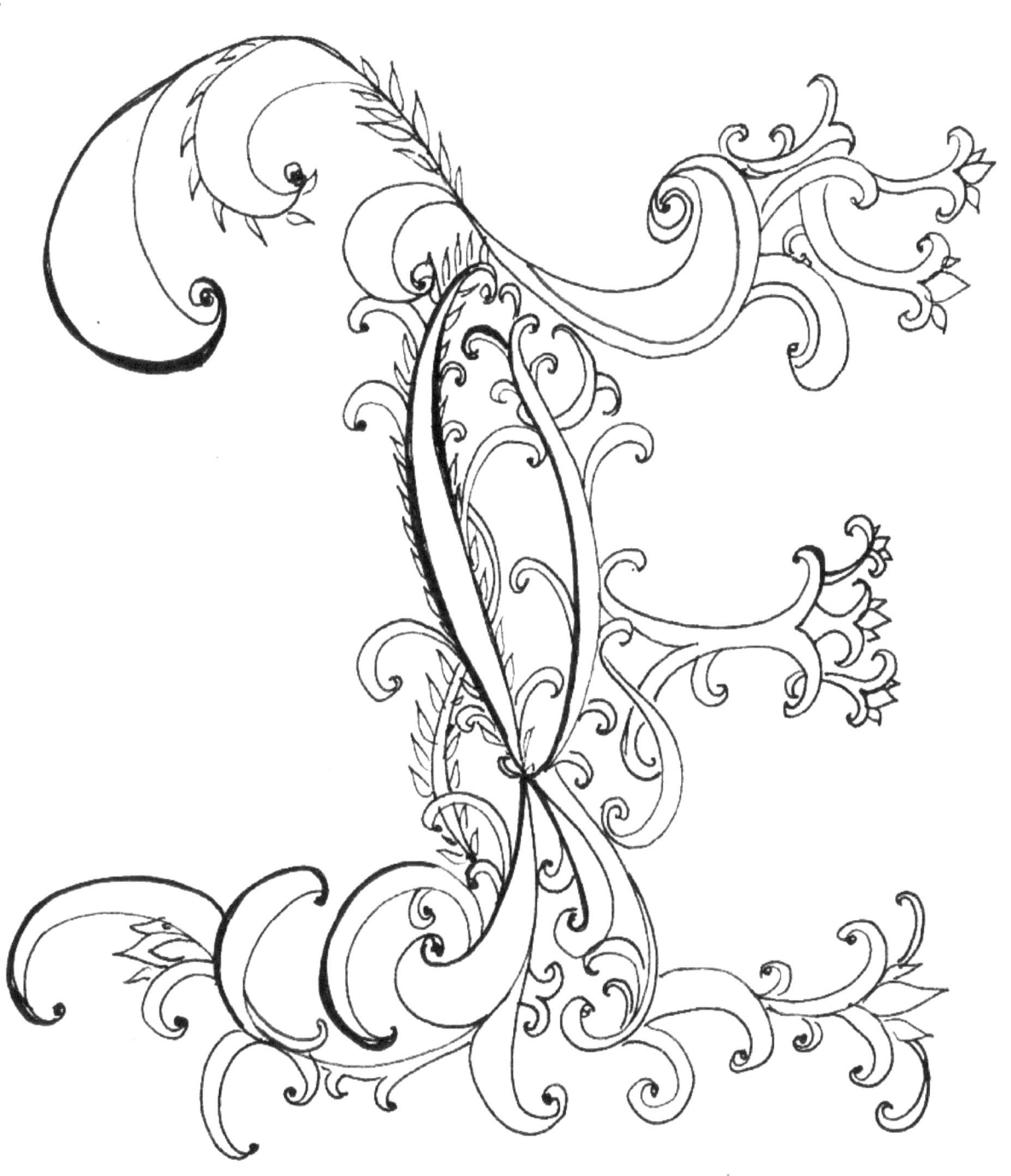

PLP c.

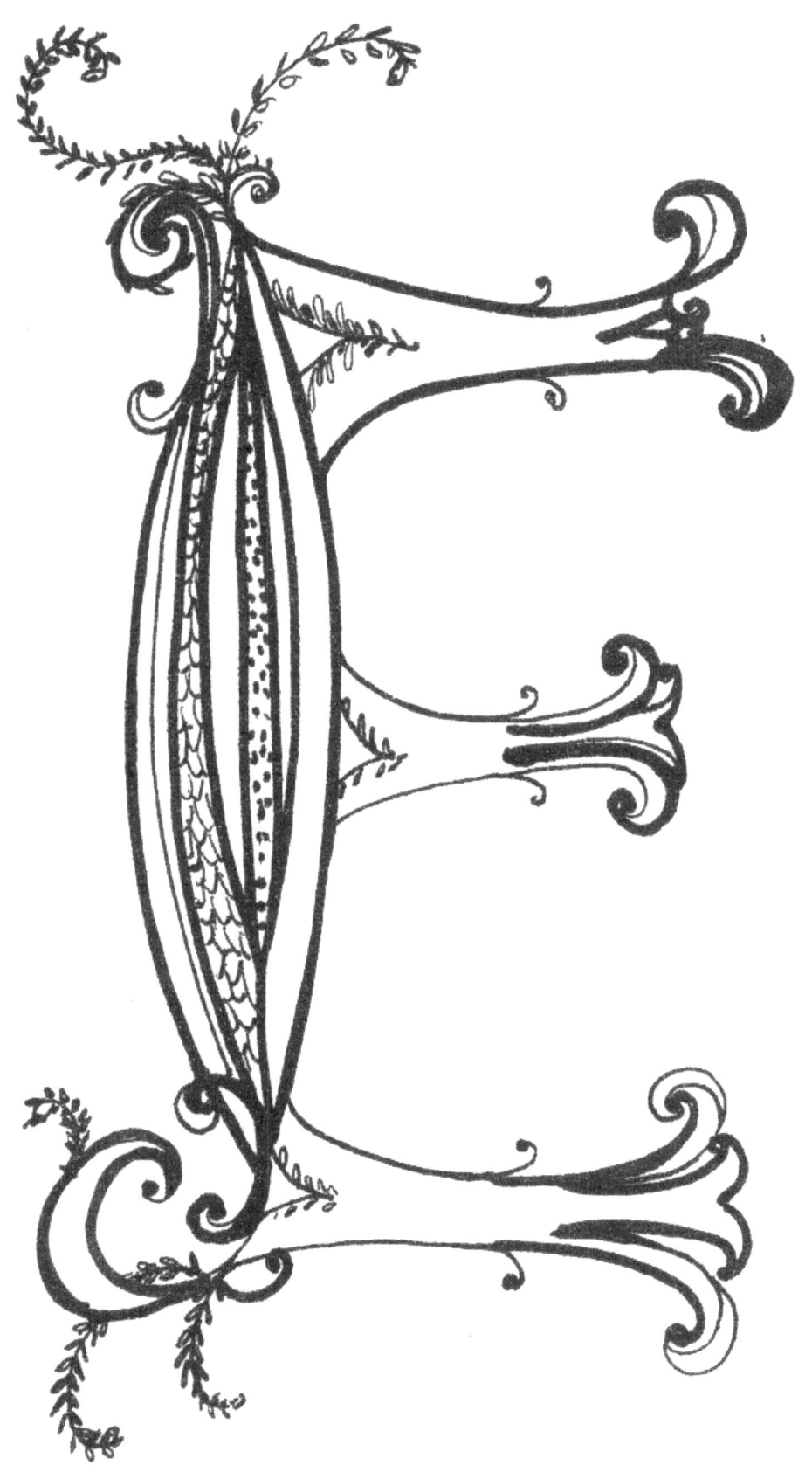

PLP
2013

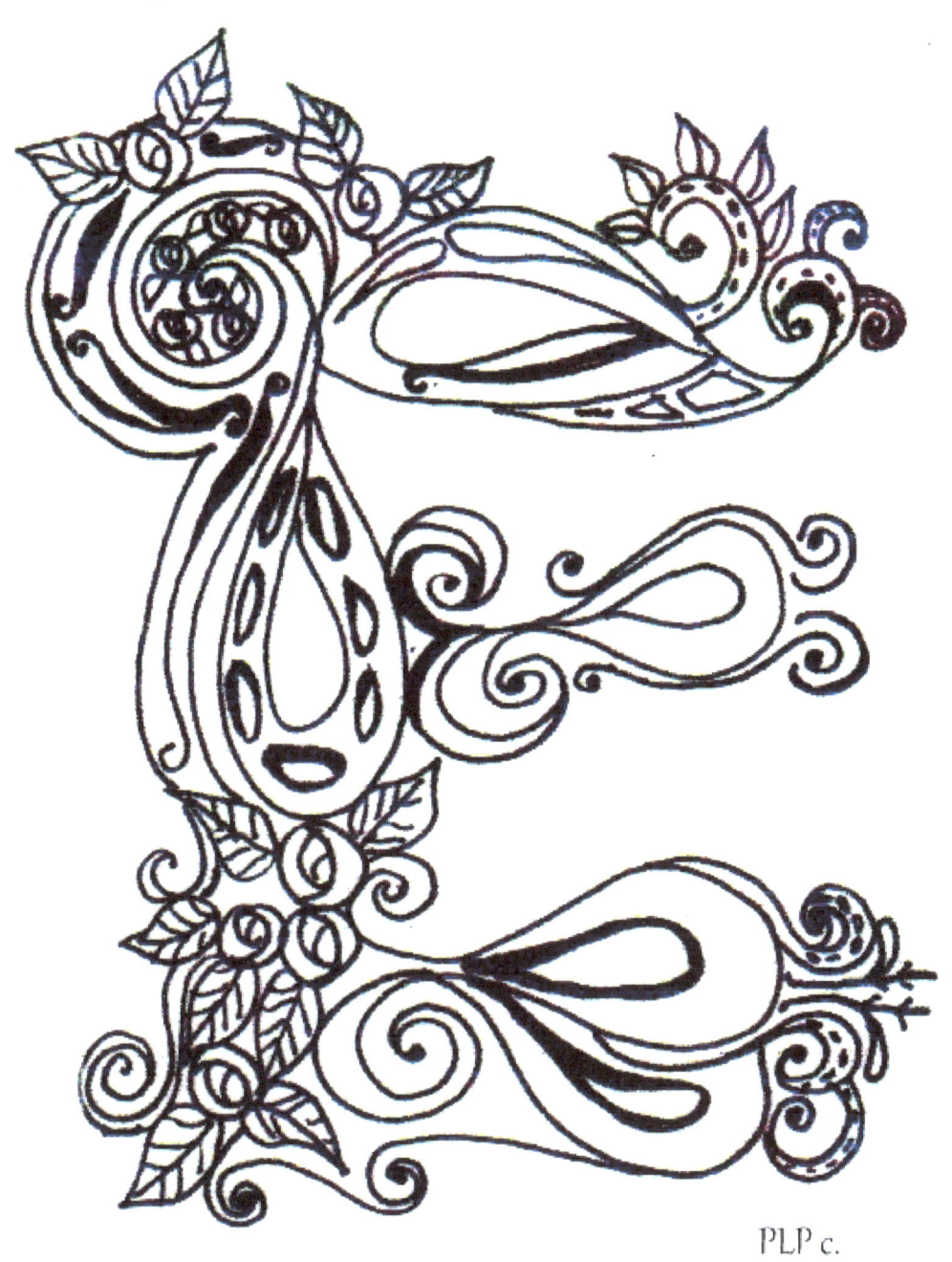

PLP c.

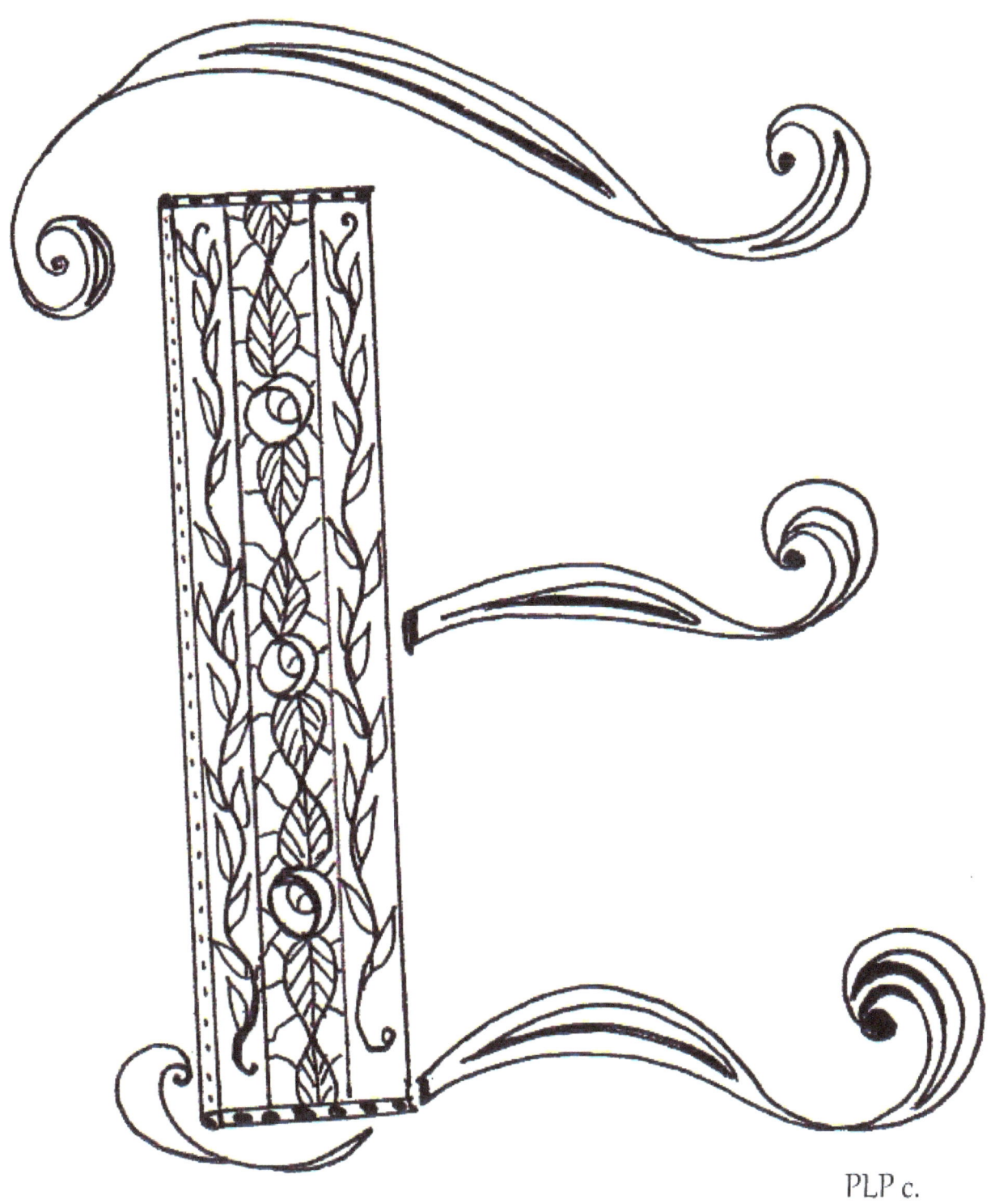

PLP c.

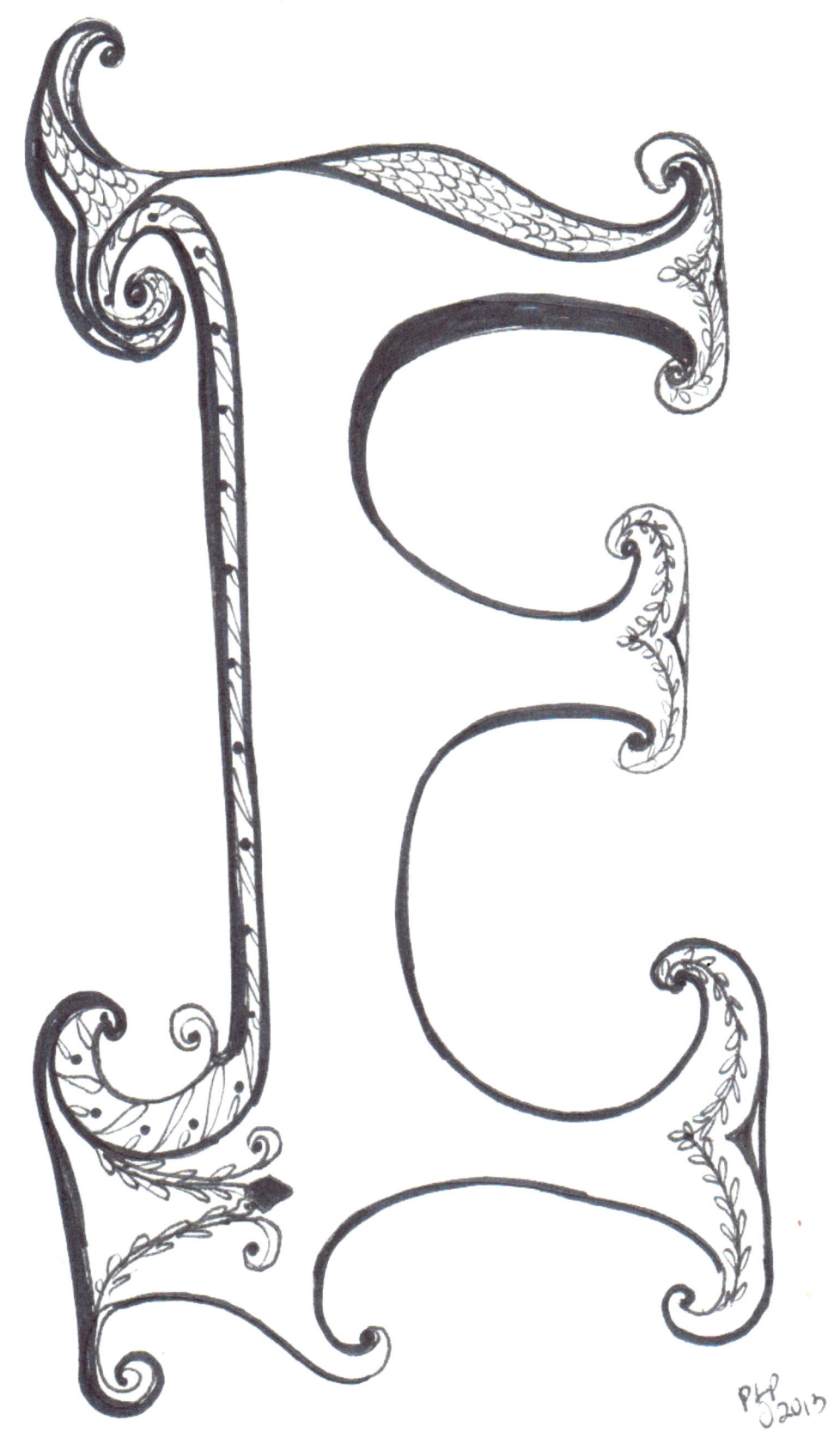

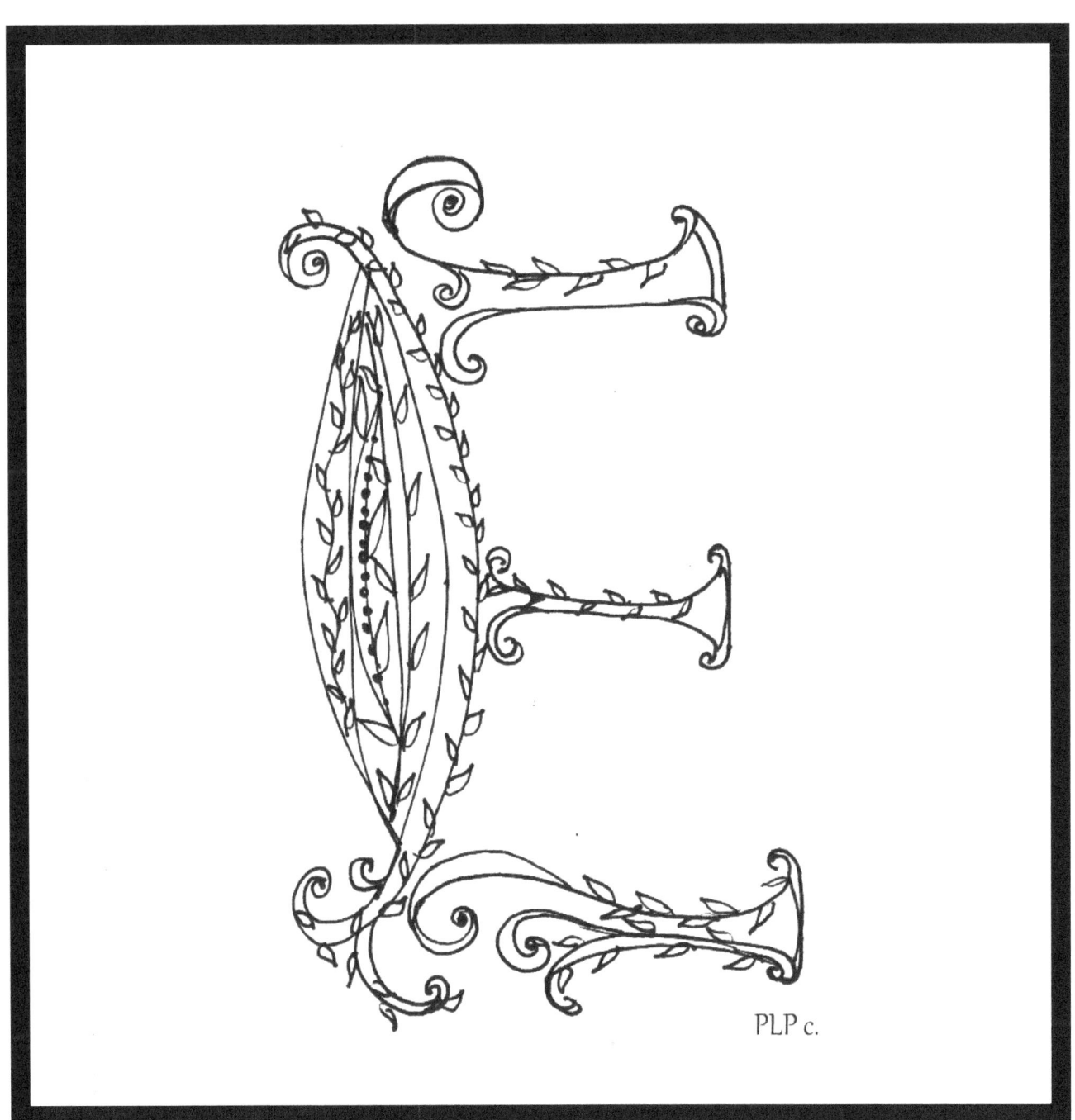

PLP c.

Isn't the letter E beautiful in a name.

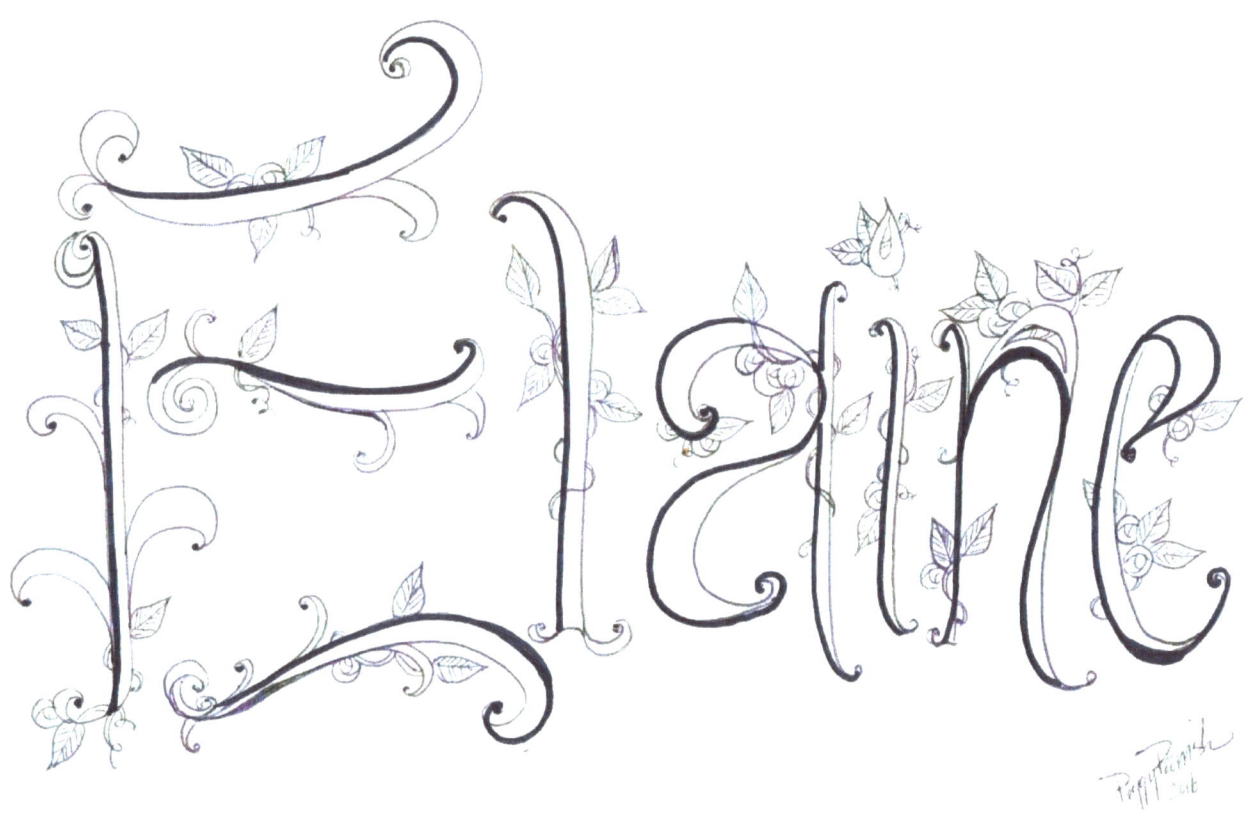

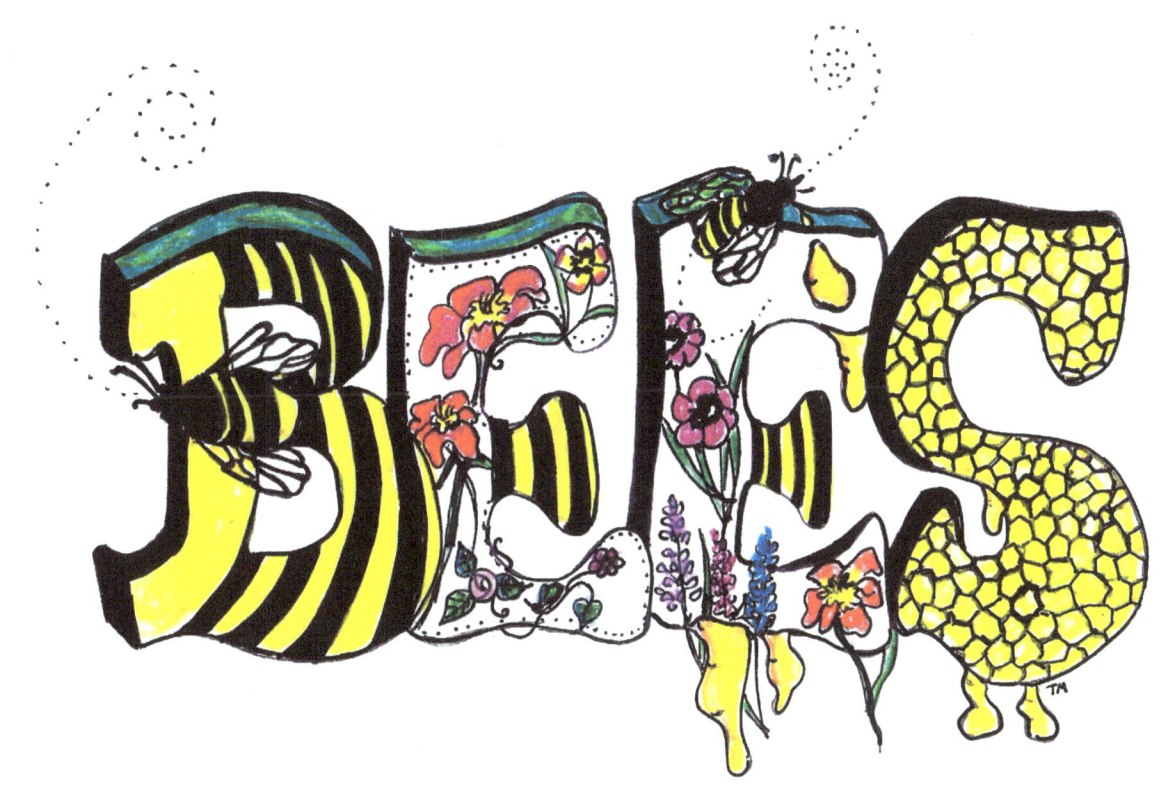

WORLD

Look how much fun the Letter E can have.

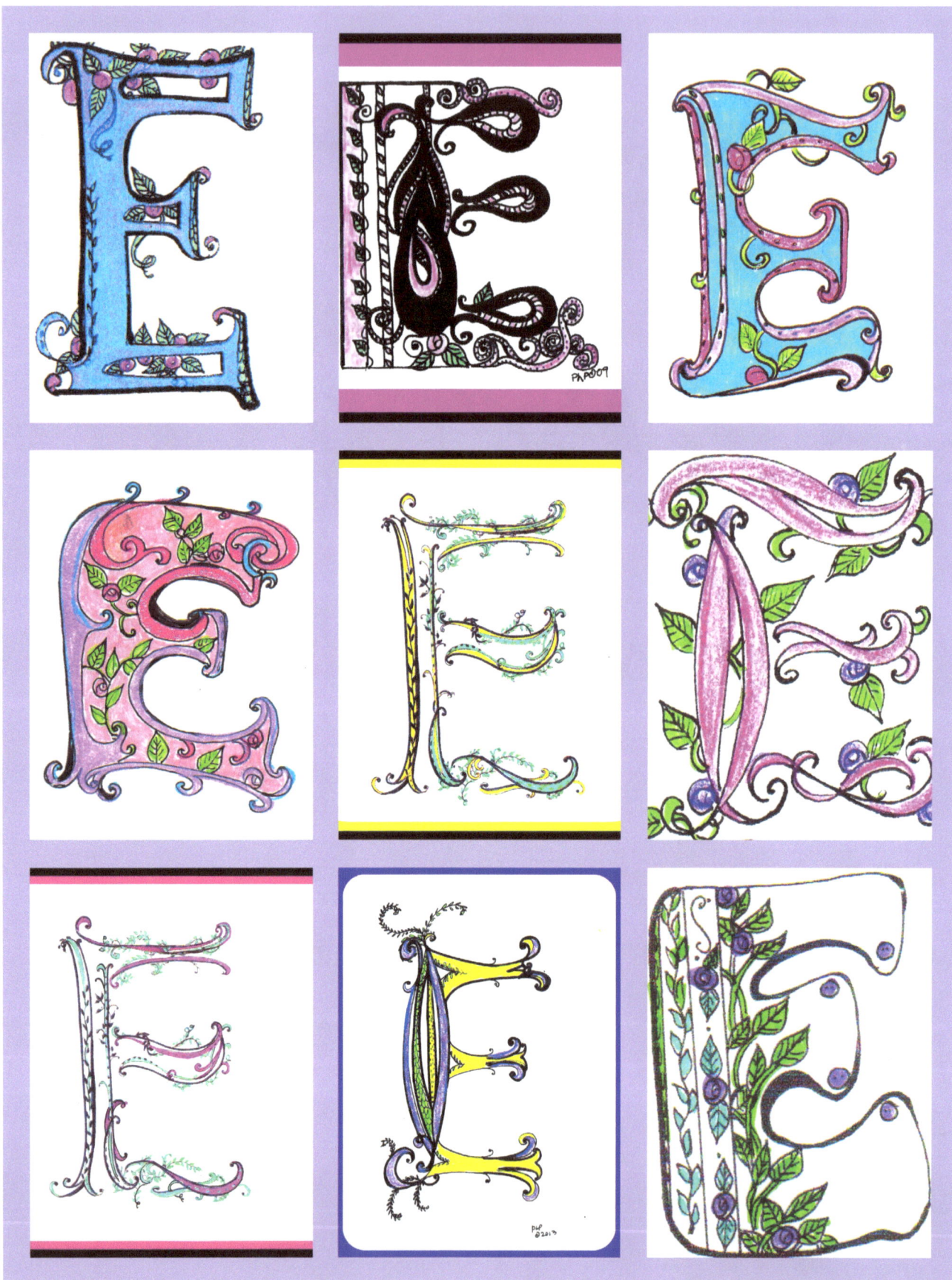